PATIENCE PAYS OFF

PATIENCE PAYS OFF

JAMES R. SHERMAN

Pathway Books

First Edition, July, 1987
Copyright © 1987 James R. Sherman
All Rights Reserved

Library of Congress Catalog Number
87-062215

International Standard Book Number
0-935538-09-7

Third Printing

Pathway Books
700 Parkview Terrace
Golden Valley, Minnesota 55416
(612) 377-1521

To: Lincoln and Renee

CONTENTS

ROUND IV
YOUR PLAN OF ACTION

PREFACE

At age 22 a young man from Illinois failed in the grocery business. The next year he ran for the state legislature and lost. He went back into business and failed again. He ran again for the legislature and won. The next year his sweetheart died. One year later, when he was 27, he suffered a nervous breakdown. Two years later he was defeated as speaker of the state House of Representatives. At 31 he ran for the post of elector and lost. At 34 he ran for the U. S. Congress and lost. He ran again 3 years later and won. But when he ran for reelection at age 39 he lost his seat. At 46 he ran for the U. S. Senate and lost. The next year he ran for Vice President and lost. Then he ran again for the Senate and lost again. Finally, at age 51, Abraham Lincoln was elected the 16th president of the United States.

Alexander Graham Bell offered exclusive rights to his new invention to Western Union. But they turned him down and rejected his telephone, saying, "What use could this company have of an electrical toy?"

Chester Carlson tried to interest Kodak in his invention, but they couldn't see any use for it. Finally, after years of rejection, Carlson convinced the Haloid Company to join him in manufacturing and marketing the device. They called the new company the Xerox Corporation.

George Lucas had to put up his own money to film *Star Wars*. By the time he finished the movie, he was broke and dispirited. Nobody wanted to buy the rights to the picture or to the sequels, so he had to keep them all himself.

I've been writing and publishing books for almost eight years. And during that period, I've had a lot of ups and downs. At times it looked like

I didn't have a snowball's chance in hell of making a go of it. But whenever I got close to throwing in the towel, I'd stop and think about people like Lincoln, Bell, Carlson, and Lucas; people who held on to their dreams and became extremely successful in their chosen fields. Their experiences have inspired me to stick to my guns and keep my dreams alive.

I'm convinced that patience, persistence, and perseverance are the primary ingredients of success. And there is no doubt in my mind that patience is the most powerful of the three. It also produces the greatest payoff.

Patience pays off in terms of greater happiness, peace of mind, and enriched self-esteem. It guarantees greater satisfaction of goals and objectives and significantly improves social, economic, and psychological well-being.

The payoff is yours for the asking if you read this book, do what it says, and refer to it whenever you feel like calling it quits.

This book will do three things for you: (1) it will help you understand how impatience can keep you from reaching your goals of success, (2) it will show you how you can recognize your own impatient behavior, and (3) it will introduce you to some easy-to-learn methods for becoming even more patient and successful than you are right now.

You will find, as you go through this book, that patience is the single, most important contributor to a happy and prosperous life. Once you commit yourself to becoming a patient person, you'll start opening doors and traveling pathways that you never dreamed existed. Just work hard, believe in what you're doing, and pay heed to some simple, straightforward techniques.

The techniques you'll find here are based on my experiences and on the experiences of a lot of very successful people. I've studied their lives, read their works, and then put their techniques together in a method that has helped me reach many of my long-term goals and objectives. I know it will do the same for you.

You're off to a good start. As long as you keep going at a steady pace, you'll make some very significant changes in the way you do things. Then, as soon as you start reaping the rewards of your efforts, tell me about your accomplishments. I'd enjoy hearing from you.

James R. Sherman, Ph.D.

ROUND I

How many times have you said, "To hell with it!" and given up on some dream you had? When have you quit a job, ended a romance, dropped out of school, or given up on a business venture because you couldn't wait to see the results you wanted?

Millions of people have fallen short of their dreams of success because they got tired of waiting. That might not seem like a major problem until you consider how much they missed out on. Their impatience kept them from reaching rewards that could very easily have been theirs.

If you're like most people, you want to be successful. But sometimes you get frustrated, because things don't always work out the way you want them to. You not only get upset over little day-to-day setbacks, but you also lose your patience when major hopes and aspirations are delayed. That really bothers you. If it didn't bother you, you wouldn't be reading this book.

Impatience is a lousy trait that can cause stress, anxiety, hypertension, and respiratory problems. It can even kill you if you let it get out of hand. But what it does most is keep you from reaching the goals and objectives that hold the greatest promise for a successful future.

This book will help you become a patient person again. It shouldn't be hard for you to get back in the groove, because you're already motivated. All you need are a few good suggestions that will show you how to stop being impatient and start being successful.

A METHOD

Here are four key directives that will help you understand and apply

1

the material that's contained in this book. Don't hesitate to elaborate on any one of the four or to add your own ideas wherever you think they're appropriate.

1. *Recognize Problems:* Take a moment right now and try to remember some of the problems you've created whenever you've lost your patience. Turn to page 3 and write down things you did or said that you now regret. This recall exercise should reinforce your desire to eliminate impatient behavior.

2. *Identify Causes of Impatience:* Try to figure out what things have caused you to become frustrated, angry, and impatient. Write those causes down on page 4. If you can't write anything down right now, wait until you get into the next section of the book where you'll find several different causes. Then come back to this list and write down those that have given you the most headaches. Once you know what the causes are, you'll know what you have to do to make the necessary changes in your behavior.

3. *Ferret Out Demons:* Turn to page 5 and make a list of things that tend to drive you up a wall. Put down things like heavy traffic, long lines, or apathetic bureaucrats. Think about them as you write them down. Try to zero in on the ones that effect you the most. They are the ones you want to watch out for, so you can disarm them before they can do any damage.

4. *Seek Solutions:* Figure out what you're going to do to take the teeth out of the major causes of your impatience. Go to page 6 and write down methods *you* think will help the most to change your behavior. Then compare your list with the techniques that are described in Round III. If you can come up with a combined list of solutions by the time you turn the final page, you'll have taken a gigantic step toward reaching your dreams of success.

Study your lists of problems, causes, demons, and solutions from time to time and add to them whenever you can. Keep thinking up ways of getting rid of your impatient behavior. Stay primed for material that will help you as you move ahead.

PROBLEMS I'VE CREATED BY BECOMING IMPATIENT

Make a list of things you said or did—after you lost your patience—that you now regret.

_____

_____

_____

_____

_____

_____

_____

_____

_____

_____

_____

_____

_____

_____

_____

THINGS THAT CAUSE ME TO LOSE MY PATIENCE

Make a list of circumstances, situations, and conditions that cause you to lose your patience more often than any others.

_____

_____

_____

_____

_____

_____

_____

_____

_____

_____

_____

_____

_____

THINGS THAT DRIVE ME UP A WALL

Make a list of irritants or pet peeves that regularly drive you up a wall.

_____

_____

_____

_____

_____

_____

_____

_____

_____

_____

_____

_____

_____

_____

_____

_____

THINGS I CAN DO TO BECOME A PATIENT PERSON

Make a list of things you can start doing right now to become a more patient person.

_____

_____

_____

_____

_____

_____

_____

_____

_____

_____

_____

_____

_____

THE PAYOFF

The payoff from all of this is success. For you, that may mean making a lot of money, having a happy marriage, earning a college degree, gaining recognition for something you've accomplished, or building a small business into a profitable enterprise.

Success means different things to different people. Some people bask in success, others fail miserably in everything they do. Some come within inches of reaching their dreams, only to fall disappointingly short of their target. And some people never get within a country mile of success because they don't know how to reach it.

You can be successful if you're willing to work for it. But in order to make it last, you're going to have to develop the one trait that will keep it going. That trait is patience.

THE ESSENCE OF PATIENCE

Patience is a state of inner tranquility that lets you respond to your environment in a calm, cool, and collected way. Patience helps you withstand pain, delay, hardship, annoyance, misfortune, or provocation with calm and fortitude and without anger, frustration, or complaint. The Roman poet Plautus suggested that, "Patience is the best remedy for every trouble."

Patience is *not* grim resignation. It's persistent striving toward a hoped-for level of success. There is as much difference between genuine patience and sullen endurance as there is between a loving smile and the malicious gnashing of teeth.

Patient people are models of confidence and self-control. They feel good about themselves and the things they do, especially when the results of their toils remain unspoiled by anger and frustration.

Patience strengthens your spirit and gives you courage and endurance in your fight against procrastination. Being patient means not saying or doing things in the height of battle that can come back to haunt you later.

Patience makes it easier for you to come up with good decisions, creative ideas, and effective ways of organizing and managing business, household, and professional activities.

Nothing demonstrates the power of patience more than the willingness of people to get involved in tediously slow-paced activities that must be completed before a goal can be reached.

You see this characteristic in the parent teaching a child, in the surgeon performing a delicate operation, or in the psychologist restoring a person's self-esteem. It is the hallmark of patience and the major characteristic of a successful person.

Nothing stands in greater contrast to the power of patience than the lousy habit of being impatient.

IMPATIENCE

Impatience is characterized by restlessness and an intense desire for relief or change. It reflects intolerance of anything that prevents the immediate satisfaction of a need.

Impatient people are often described as being those who change cars, jobs, houses, and spouses at will. They eat fast foods when they dine out. And when they eat at home, they pop fast-frozen dinners into their microwave ovens so they can watch fast-action TV.

Impatient voters and anxious newscasters can't wait to see who the victors are, so elections are often decided way before the polls even open.

Impatient people abandon long-term goals in preference for a quick fix. College students who complain of Mickey Mouse requirements, quickly tire of the drudgery of their studies and drop out of school in pursuit of an easier life. Husbands and wives hasten to file for divorce rather than confront the day-to-day challenges that test their marriage. Young executives quickly discard their career goals in the face of difficult long-term requirements for success. Anxious entrepreneurs jump ship as soon as their fledgling enterprises run into cash-flow problems.

At their worst, impatient people are driven by a reckless desire for rapid change. Their crazy, madcap race to do something different, or get someplace else in a hurry, becomes — for all too many of them — a frenzied way of life.

Unfortunately, society encourages and reinforces much of this impatient behavior. You can see it every day in movies, television, and advertising. And, as you have probably noticed, those messages do not go unheeded.

The more patient *you* can become, the more aware you'll be of the impatient people around you who drive like maniacs, hate to stand in line, and get mad when other people are late. You'll find these fussbudgets to be characteristically hostile, irritable, and intolerant. They get all riled up over delays, blame others for their misfortunes, and allow petty annoyances to drive them up a wall. The impatient behavior you see on the surface is just a hint of much deeper problems. The frustration and anger that impatient people direct toward their normal day-to-day activities is the same frustration and anger that screws up their career goals, personal relationships, and general wellbeing. As a result, many of these fretful people have shaky marriages, are unhappy about their jobs, suffer from high blood pressure, and have a helluva time staying on a diet.

You're probably wondering why so many people act this way, given the lousy things that can happen to them. Here are some of the reasons.

THE ROOTS OF IMPATIENCE

Almost all behavior is generated by people's needs, wants, and desires. If people are hungry, need companionship, or seek a successful position in life, they do what they have to do to meet those needs. Problems develop when an obstacle gets in the way and prevents them from achieving their goals and objectives. Most people get irritated when that happens.

The blocking of a need spurs some people onward and upward with even greater purpose and zeal. With their shoulders to the wheel and their noses to the grindstone, these high-achievers stick to their guns until they have successfully reached their goals. That kind of enthusiasm is sometimes misinterpreted as impatience. But the difference is really easy to see.

Impatient people get frustrated and angry. Instead of rolling up their sleeves and moving ahead with greater resolve, these soreheads throw in the towel and quit. Their aspirations for success, though noble in the beginning, wither and die like daisies in the desert.

You have to work hard and believe in what you're doing to become a patient person. But once you've done it, you've opened up some fabulous opportunities for being successful.

WHAT'S AHEAD

Now it's time to take another step on the road to success. Turn to Round II. That's where you'll discover some interesting things about yourself and this good for nothing habit you're trying to get rid of.

ROUND II

This is the section of the book in which you will find some of the major causes of impatient behavior. Read through each description carefully and try to get a good picture in your mind's eye of the kinds of behavior that are discussed. Just remember that people react in different ways, so these may not be exact accounts of how you behave in similar situations. That's okay, because you're looking for ideas, not precise characterizations.

Go back to page 4 from time to time and work on your list of causes. Come up with a new list if it provides a better description of your behavior. Add any causes you can think of that aren't dealt with here.

Take a minute now and turn to page 12. Make a list of situations where you *never* lose your patience. Look at the people involved and try to figure out why you're patient with them and not with others. Look for contrasts between situations where you never lose your cool and those you listed back on page 5. Why do you suppose you lose your patience in some situations and not others? Keep these questions in mind as you go through this section and see if you can come up with some answers on your own.

IN THE BEGINNING

The word patience comes from the Latin word *pati*, meaning to suffer or endure hardship. It's what Minnesota Viking fans have gone through for years.

Patient people can put up with just about anything, especially when they're trying very hard to satisfy some basic need. Impatient people, on

11

SITUATIONS IN WHICH I NEVER LOSE MY PATIENCE

Make a list of situations where you always stay calm, cool, and collected.

_____

_____

_____

_____

_____

_____

_____

_____

_____

_____

_____

_____

_____

_____

the other hand, get all riled up when their needs are blocked. A common character trait of impatient people is their unwillingness to suffer any kind of discomfort while waiting for their desires to be satisfied. Lack of patience not only puts the kibosh on one's ability to move ahead, it also takes away the zest for living. It leaves in its wake failure, disappointment, and unhappiness. Especially for those who can see what their impatient behavior has cost them. They're left with empty dreams and nagging thoughts of what might have been had they waited out the storm.

Impatience is a killer. Cemeteries are crowded with lead-footed drivers who were in too big a hurry as they sped to their destination. And lying next to them are the high-fliers who died from the effects of stress and hypertension that were brought on by the two most common sources of impatience: anger and frustration.

People who start out being patient often run into trouble as soon as they come up against an obstacle of some kind.

OBSTACLES

When viewed objectively, most obstacles are nothing more than common roadblocks. But sometimes they seem to be insurmountable. Some obstacles like social, psychological, or financial restraints occur naturally. Others seem to pop up out of nowhere.

Here is a list of common obstacles that you might have run into from time to time. Feel free to add any others you can think of that aren't listed here.

1. *Environmental obstacles:* blizzards, typhoons, road detours, traffic tie-ups, people standing in line.
2. *Psychological obstacles:* fear, anxiety, anger, frustration.
3. *Biological obstacles:* age, sex, physical or mental handicaps.
4. *Social obstacles:* laws, taboos, social customs, house rules.

You're bound to run into obstacles like these at sometime or another no matter what you're doing. And every one of them has the potential for slowing you down, restricting you, or cutting you off at the pass as you dash toward the finish line.

Whenever you run into one of these obstacles, you probably react the way a lot of other people do. You call upon some old habits that you've been developing since the day you were born. The first thing patient people do when they run into an obstacle is try to remove it. If that doesn't work, they back up and start over. Or they try to hurdle, skirt, or modify the obstacle in some way. If all else fails and patient people still can't get past the obstacle, they modify their goals to make them more realistic. Then they head off in another direction and leave the obstacle behind.

Impatient people take a much different approach. Instead of taking an objective look at the obstacle and trying to figure out how to deal with it, they talk themselves into getting frustrated and angry. Many of them abandon their goals entirely. Others try to blow the obstacle out of the water rather than seek some kind of compromise.

The one thing that triggers this impatient behavior more than anything else is frustration.

FRUSTRATION

The first thing most people do when they run into an obstacle is tell themselves that something is wrong. Things just aren't the way they're supposed to be, and they're going to have to do something about it. But instead of doing something rational, many people just get frustrated.

Some people get frustrated at the drop of a hat, even when they see a naturally-occuring obstacle well ahead of time. Other people only get frustrated when an obstacle jumps out at them unexpectedly.

Patient people are able to defuse their frustration so it doesn't affect their progress toward a goal. They follow the advice of Seneca, the Roman stoic and philosopher who told his followers to "Accustom yourself to that which you bear ill, and you will bear it well."

You probably got frustrated once or twice when things didn't go your way. But like most people, you probably didn't stay frustrated for very long. And your short-term frustration probably didn't have much effect on your long-term goals.

Unfortunately, that's not what happens to people who have a habit of losing their patience. Their frustration usually turns to anger, hostility, and the need to get even. They want to take somebody's head off.

RETALIATION

Anger, hostility, and the need to retaliate are common byproducts of big-time, self-imposed frustration.

The first thing many impatient people do when they're angry is replace their desire to reach a goal with an immediate need to get even. As soon as the wheels of anger start turning, they launch into a sequence of retaliatory actions against the person or situation that gets blamed for making an obstacle appear.

If retaliation is slow in coming, impatient people will get even more frustrated. And since they don't function very well when they're angry, their retaliatory behavior will create additional obstacles. That compounds their frustration and makes them even more upset.

Frustrated people generally start feeling guilty when they see how worthless their anger is. Their guilt lowers their self-esteem and makes them even more anxious to accomplish something. But if their desperate need to get something done leads to more obstacles, frustration, and hostility, then these unfortunate people could stay on their merry-go-round until hell freezes over.

If the need to retaliate can sidetrack normal day-to-day responsibilities, you can bet the farm that it will completely derail more substantial things like business careers, college goals, and personal relationships.

Impatient people who rely on bad habits to cope with minor obstacles are bound to use them again when the needs are significant and the obstacles are formidable. If they start foaming at the mouth in a traffic jam, they'll go into orbit when their careers get stonewalled.

If people can learn to cope with garden-variety obstacles without getting angry or frustrated, they'll have far fewer problems when the roof caves in.

They'll be as calm, cool, and collected when making difficult business decisions as they are in rush-hour traffic. They'll be as considerate with their close, personal friends as they are with people who make them stand in line at the post office.

St. Francis of Assisi, the celebrated Italian monk and founder of the Order of Franciscans, recognized this trait among patient people. "Where there is patience and humility," he said, "there is neither anger nor vexation."

Look around you at the patient people you know. They may get their danders up once in a while like everybody else, but they don't make a habit of it. And dollars to doughnuts says they're not letting unnecessary emotional responses keep them from being successful.

The difference between people who frequently get angry and frustrated, and those who never seem to lose their patience, can often be determined by how confused they are about what they're trying to do.

CONFUSION

Watch someone try to put together a child's toy without looking at the directions, or ride with someone who's trying to drive to a strange destination without looking at a road map, and you'll see a major cause of impatience.

These people have a fairly good idea of where they want to go and what they want to do, but they don't have the vaguest idea about how to do it. That bothers them. But instead of taking the time to figure out the right way to reach their objective, they stumble along like mice in a maze, looking for shortcuts and making a lot of dumb mistakes. And those dumb mistakes usually stir up a whole bunch of obstacles that cause them to become even more frustrated.

Some people will recognize how, when, where, and why they screwed up. They'll stop, look at the directions, read the map, and figure out what they have to do to get back on track. Eventually, they'll reach their goal.

Others won't admit they're in trouble. Or they won't take the time to see how they messed up. They'll stay confused. And then they'll throw the toy out the window, tear up the road map, and call it quits. It's a typical response that gets repeated time after time. And more often than not, these people's dreams of success end up deader than a politician's promise.

Some people, even when they know what they're supposed to do, have a hard time deciding what should be done first.

LACK OF PRIORITIES

Some people find it hard to distinguish between petty annoyances and major crises. They either don't know how to make the distinctions, or they don't want to take the time to figure out what's important and what's not.

They lose their patience at the drop of a hat and seem to be perpetually agitated about everything. They have no sense of priority. If you've ever traveled by air, you've probably seen some of these fussbudgets at their worst.

They crowd the gate so they can be the first to board, even when their seats have been assigned ahead of time. Once they're seated, they fret and stew about everything; the food, the service, the departure time, and any delays they encounter along the way. When the plane reaches its destination, they bolt down the aisle and dash into the terminal so they can stand around for an hour and wait for their luggage.

They're just as unsettled at home. They switch their TV sets on and off, change the channels, and swear a lot because their favorite programs don't come on when they want them to.

They'll walk out of a doctor's office, no matter how important the appointment is, because they don't like waiting.

Learning when to hurry takes as much discipline as learning when to wait. Even successful people will get frustrated and lose their patience when things don't go the way they want them to. But at least they know enough not to get cranked up about things that aren't important.

Some people have no problem recognizing the importance of their tasks, but they get antsy whenever they think about tackling them.

COLD FEET

Hesitancy and doubt are common problems for people who pursue elusive dreams of success. But sometimes these irritations lead to irrational assessments and an urgent need to get out of a testy situation as quickly as possible.

Insecure people get frustrated and lose their patience when their hoped-for results don't show up at the time they expect them to. The more frustrated they get, the harder it is for them to accurately judge where they are and how well they're doing. They get anxious and wonder if they're really doing the right thing.

Some people question their ability to finish what they started. Others worry about what their friends and neighbors will say if their dreams of success end in failure.

A few of these people are in over their heads, but others have just lost their courage. They feel trapped by the commitments they've made and they're looking for a way out. Frustration has muddied up their perspective so much that they can no longer see anything positive in what they're doing. These anxious people need to reaffirm their strengths and weaknesses. They need to take another look at the goals they've set for themselves. They need to see if they're still on the right track. But instead of dealing directly with hesitancy and doubt, many of them opt for escape. And as they dive for cover, they dump their goals and aspirations like loaves of day-old bread.

If these people were to stay in the fray any longer, they would probably become paralyzed by fear. That's another cause of impatience.

FEAR

A lot of people get scared whenever they find an unfamiliar obstacle in their path. The obstacle can be an interview with a stranger, an unexpected assignment, or a challenge to their system of values.

They don't really know what they're afraid of, because they never get close enough to the obstacle to get a good look at it. But they still recognize the obstacle as a potential threat to the satisfaction of their needs.

Their fear leads to frustration and impatience, followed by a mad scramble to get away from the apparition that stands before them. Their pell-mell behavior stems from anxieties and phobias that in many cases are exaggerated, unexplained, or just flat-out illogical.

Some people are afraid of strangers or of long lines of people. Some are afraid of being confined or of being pressed upon by other people's demands. Others are afraid of not being liked, of being rejected by their peers, or of being left behind. There are also those who are afraid of failure or of looking like a complete klutz in the eyes of others.

The fears that keep impatient people from reaching their dreams of success usually reside in the deep, dark corners of their minds. Until those fears are rooted out and done away with, they will lie in those dark places, unchallenged and unresolved. And the impatient people who harbor those fears will never gain the courage to climb the ladder of success.

That's unfortunate. Because most fears, when brought out into the light of discovery, will dry up and blow away. All it takes is a little courage, self-evaluation, and the determination to stop procrastinating and do it.

Fear has many close relatives. Lack of self-confidence is one that ranks as a major cause of impatience.

LACK OF SELF-CONFIDENCE

Some people are driven by an insatiable need to improve their self-confidence. They try to accomplish this goal by being out in front of everybody else. They try to be the first to finish a conversation, the first to get through a door, the first to get out of a parking lot, and the first in line for every event they attend.

They think that being ahead of everyone else has enormous prestige value. But in most cases, their pushy, aggressive, and impatient behavior has the opposite effect. It turns people off.

These anxious people are left with even greater feelings of insecurity because of the negative responses they get. But instead of backing off and trying to improve their character, many of them come on even stronger. They try to get other people to think they're wonderful, and in doing so, hope to gain the self-respect they so desperately need.

Some impatient people get so wrapped up in trying to improve their self-image that they allow their dreams of success to become contests in which they must be declared the winner.

COMPETITIVENESS

Some people are obsessed with the need to compete against real or imagined opponents. If there's no competition, there's no motivation. If they don't see themselves as being in a win-loss situation, they get out before their goals are even formulated.

These highly competitive people refuse to accept ties or second-place finishes no matter how hard they work or how well they perform. They can't co-exist with their peers, they have to defeat them.

If they see any obstacles to their competitive advantage, or if they feel in any way that they're dropping behind their real or imagined opponents, their patience will disappear and they'll jump ship for easier prey. Whatever goals they had at the beginning will be cast aside like dead fish.

No matter how much potential these people have for success, they will only use it when they're assured of coming out better than somebody else. They need to be in control.

THE NEED FOR CONTROL

Most people like to have control over their destiny. But for some, the need for control goes beyond self-control and extends to the control of other people and situations.

Attempts at control can involve direct action, like passing another car, cutting in line, or dragging someone across the street against their will.

It can also be displayed indirectly with a frown, a heavy sigh, whistling, or drumming of fingers.

Impatient people get frustrated and angry when their attempts at control are unsuccessful, or if the results come later than expected. Before long, a habitual pattern of impatient behavior develops in which control and rapid closure are viewed as major outcomes.

People who aggressively try to control everything that effects their long-term objectives don't realize how many variables they're dealing with. When they eventually discover that they're not in the driver's seat, they quickly drop what they're doing and move on to something else. College goals, career choices, personal relationships, and other aspirations are all cut down before they can bear fruit.

People who aggressively seek control mistakenly assume that they have gained some advantage over the people they passed, yelled at, or hung up on. But not so. The victims of their rude behavior may tolerate them for a while, but in the long run they usually throw the rascals out.

Ironically, this behavior, by it's very nature, epitomizes a *lack* of control. It's usually supplemented by the need to get everything done as quickly as possible.

THE NEED FOR RAPID CLOSURE

Many impatient people are driven by a desperate need to close things off as fast as they can, whether they've achieved a satisfactory solution or not. If their dreams of success are not met quickly, they'll cast away their current goals and objectives along with a lot of other unfulfilled aspirations.

Impatient people display their need for closure in spontaneous and insignificant events like side-stepping a traffic tie-up, passing a slow moving car, cutting in line at the movies, hanging up on a caller, or completing a cross-country trip in record time without stopping for rest or meals.

In a deeper sense, impatient people act the same way toward more significant events in their lives. They try to get firm commitments from others whether the relationships have matured or not. Career choices must be satisfied as quickly as possible, according to their expectations, or the careers are abandoned.

Entrepreneurs and small-business operators often fall into the trap of expecting too much too soon. Those who allow frustration and impatience to cloud their vision, usually find their hopes for success have died without a prayer.

Impatient people never seem to follow a steady, unimpeded path toward a goal. They're usually running off half-cocked in a dozen different directions, trying to put out fires that they often start themselves. Their manic sense of urgency is the main cause of their impatience.

People who think only about getting things done have little regard for direction or purpose. The only thing that really counts is completion. They seldom take the time to do things right because they're always in a hurry. So the results they end up with are almost always incomplete, meaningless, or of poor quality. It's no wonder they're dissatisfied and always looking for change.

Whenever these hyperactive people encounter an obstacle, they cast aside their goals and objectives without even taking the time to get frustrated. They justify their hasty exits by saying that the task wasn't worth the time they had already spent on it.

These people never slow down long enough to figure out what they have to do to become successful. Many of them wear themselves out before they ever have a chance to amount to anything.

One thing is certain. These people could never survive in a steady, unchanging, and montonous environment.

MONOTONY

A lot of people lose their patience over things that are tedious, slow-paced, and dreadfully dull, even if they're essential to the fulfillment of a significant goal.

Many of life's greatest challenges are made up in part of tediously uniform tasks that have to be finished before a larger goal can be reached. If those tasks cannot easily be changed, and if the people who face them aren't willing to compromise, then the tasks aren't going to get done, and success will remain an elusive dream.

Monotony has probably been the kiss of death for more good intentions than any other obstacle.

Scores of musicians, athletes, artisans and other skilled performers have given up their quest for excellence because they found no satisfaction in the repetitive mechanics and monotony of practice. When the tedium of their tasks began to outweigh perceived rewards, they called it quits and went on to other things.

Impatience is clearly an impediment to a better life, and it's a lousy response to reality. But it's a response that can still be changed with a little hard work and determination.

THE ROAD AHEAD

There are as many causes of impatient behavior as there are dreams of success. You've been introduced to just a few of the things that might have kept you from reaching that list of goals and objectives that you have taped to your bedroom mirror.

Now is the time to figure out why your hopes and aspirations have eluded you. The first step in that exercise is to analyze your successes and failures.

Write down on a sheet of paper all the things you've done that you're proud of. Put down everything you can think of, as long as it gave you a satisfied feeling of accomplishment. Then try to figure out why you were successful. Did you rush through each task, or did you patiently pursue it through a series of carefully-planned steps?

What about your failures? Write those down on another sheet, and take a real close look at them. Did you start out with good intentions? Where did you drop the ball? Was it because you tried to run instead of walk?

Knowing why you've missed the train is half the battle. Knowing what to do so it doesn't happen again will keep you on the road to success. If impatient behavior is the culprit, and you're willing to accept that, then make up your mind to shake that nasty habit immediately. The next section will help you do that.

Go through the techniques that are presented in Round III and tailor them to your own way of doing things. Use them every way you can to keep from losing your patience. If they can get you moving toward those goals and objectives you've always wanted, it'll be the best investment you will ever make. Do it now.

MY MOST SIGNIFICANT SUCCESSES

Make a list of things you like to remember most.

_____

_____

_____

_____

_____

_____

_____

_____

_____

_____

_____

_____

Use more paper if necessary.

MY WORST MISTAKES

Make a list of things you would rather forget about.

_____

_____

_____

_____

_____

_____

_____

_____

_____

_____

_____

_____

_____

_____

*Don't worry if you can't fill the page.

ROUND III

Getting rid of old habits and changing long-established behavior patterns isn't going to be easy. But the 23 techniques that are described in this section are going to help you make the change without too much difficulty.

Some of these techniques might not apply to your particular situation. Don't worry about it. Use the ones that do apply. Let them become an integral part of your lifestyle.

Come back later to the methods you initially passed over and see if there isn't something in them that you can use. Or better yet, use them as springboards to come up with your own techniques.

Keep a journal of your progress. Write down important things that happen to you and tell how you respond to them. Refer to your journal from time to time. You'll be pleasantly surprised to see how quickly your successes will add up.

The first technique for becoming a patient person is critical. Without it, the other techniques won't help a bit.

MAKE A COMMITMENT

Make a commitment to yourself and others that from now on, you're going to be a calm, cool, and collected person. Make it clear that you're going to meet day-to-day calamities with patience and understanding, and you're going to pursue your dreams and aspirations with persistence and perseverance.

The people to whom you make your commitment will not only applaud you for your efforts, they'll lend a helping hand whenever and wherever they can.

Any important task has a greater chance of being completed if there's a formal commitment attached to it, especially if the commitment is made in public. That's because you're more likely to keep a public commitment made to someone else than one you make in private to yourself.

Once you make a commitment to someone else, you naturally start thinking about their expectations and less about your own. The fears, concerns, and anxieties that frustrated you in the past end up being secondary to the expectations of people you feel good about. By including other people in your hopes for the future, you'll be more at ease and less likely to be provoked when you run into obstacles.

Your change in attitude alone will probably help more than anything else to keep you from losing your patience. And having others share in the pursuit of your dreams and aspirations, will make it a lot more enjoyable.

Breathe life into your commitment. Turn it into a major objective with milestones, timetables, and specific outcomes. Decide what you're going to do, when you're going to do it, and what you expect to gain by it. If you have trouble with this planning process, refer to *Plan For Success*, another book in the *DO IT! Success Series*.

The more effort you put into your commitment, the better off you'll be in the long run. Just remember that Rome wasn't built in a day and neither were you. You're not going to get rid of all your bad habits overnight. So hang in there and do the best you can. The change will come soon enough.

PRACTICE SELF-CONTROL

There is no greater source of power than self-control. If you can control your emotions, you can control your future. So tear into those emotions of frustration, anger, and hostility with the discipline of a diamond cutter.

Say "no" to the habitual temptation of getting frustrated. It will give you a feeling of control that will last for days. Apply that control to all your emotions and before you know it, you'll be successful in everything you do.

Watch for body signals. If your heart beats faster when you're in heavy traffic, slow down. If you find it harder to breathe when you're trying to get through a long line, relax. Take a deep breath and let your muscles go loose. If your pulse rate climbs when you have to wait for someone, find something else to do. If you start to sweat when you run into an obstacle, keep cool. Don't let your emotions take over your body. Just get out of the fast lane and slow down a little.

Learn to recognize and understand your moods, those conscious states of mind where your emotions sneak up and take control of your behavior. Make your moods work for you, not against you. Here's a list of hints that will help you control your moods.

• If you're in a bad mood when you start the day, stop what you're doing and change that mood to a happier one. Take off your frown and put on a smile.

• Think happy thoughts instead of angry ones. Think about a place, a person, or a thing that makes you happy.

• Tackle hard jobs when you're in a productive mood.

• Work on easy tasks when you're less motivated. Your mood will change as you finish the easy tasks and soon you'll be motivated again to tackle the hard jobs.

• Save mental tasks for a time when you're in a thinking mood.

• Don't jump into a people situation when you're in the mood to take somebody's head off.

Gaining self-control over your emotions may seem hard to do at first. But this is where you're going to have to start if you're going to stick to your commitment.

Once you've got control, you can do almost anything and do it with enthusiasm. The key to developing this technique is to picture yourself, as you go along, as being a happy, patient, and successful person.

SHARPEN YOUR PERSPECTIVE

Most people believe there are just as many ways to drive, work, or carry on a conversation as there are religions, political philosophies, or recipes for pickling pears. So don't measure your progress against rigid, uncompromising ideals. Ideals are standards of excellence that only exist in people's minds, not in reality.

That's not to say that ideals are bad. They provide excellent guidelines for behavior. But they can lead to an awful lot of frustration if you follow them blindly.

Try to view your world as it really is, not just as you'd like it to be. Look at it from other people's viewpoints as well as your own. Put it under a microscope and see what's really there. Talk to people. Read magazines and newspapers. Watch the news on TV. Look for details instead of vague impressions. Make a sincere effort to be more perceptive, tolerant, and understanding of yourself and others. Don't expect miracles from those people who haven't yet reached sainthood. Be patient if you want things to change. And remember that more people are flattered into virtue than bullied out of vice. Don't judge the play until the fat lady sings.

COMMUNICATE

Fine-tune your conversational skills, and you'll put the kibosh on a major source of impatience and frustration.

Good conversation should be a dialog, not a duel of monologues. So be a good listener. Don't try to hurry other people by finishing their sentences or interrupting their thoughts to say what you think they're saying. Let them go at their own pace. They'll get there soon enough.

Forget your prejudices. Tune in to what other people are actually saying, not to what you think you hear. Ask questions, and then be sure to remember the answers. You'll not only gain other people's knowledge, you'll also gain their respect.

It might help to follow the advice of John Wayne, one of America's greatest Western actors. He said the secret of successful acting was to "Talk low, talk slow, and don't say too much."

ANALYZE AND PLAN

You won't get so frustrated when you run into an obstacle if you know where you're going and how you're going to get there. The secret lies in four simple steps.

1. Analyze your present situation. List the steps you have to take to reach your goal, and identify any shortcomings you have that

might jeopardize your success.
2. Correct as many shortcomings as you can.
3. Identify your strengths and apply them to each step of your plan.
4. Carry out your plan as soon as possible. Do the best you can with what you have available.

Simplify your life by doing one thing at a time and developing the wherewithal to get it done.

Do the things you like to do and are good at. You'll have greater success and you'll have fun doing it.

Exercise your mind every day and keep it razor sharp. To be conscious of the fact that you missed a few tidbits of knowledge along the way is a great step toward gaining additional knowledge. Open up those brain cells and pack in all the smarts you can get your hands on.

Patience, perseverance, and persistence, along with a careful analysis of your dreams and aspirations will help you surmount every obstacle you encounter on your journey. If you venture into unfamiliar territory, take time to study the terrain. Don't be afraid to admit your ignorance if you get in over your head.

Every discovery of what is false moves you closer to the knowledge of what is true.

DEVELOP GOALS AND OBJECTIVES

Goals and objectives are the signposts of progress. Without them, you'll get lost on a trail of misery and despair.

It's amazing how many great opportunities are disguised as unsolvable problems. In the beginning, every worthwhile idea seems to be impossible. But in reality, there are few things that can't be done.

When people fail, it's not because they lack the means to succeed. They fail because they don't have the patience to figure out where they're going or how they'll get there.

You won't fail if you take the time to translate your dreams and aspirations into specific goals and objectives that you know are worth reaching.

No dream is too distant, no goal too difficult, if you pursue it with patience and persistence and face the ever-present obstacles with well-formulated plans and the willingness to work as hard as you can.

The only place where success comes before work is in the dictionary. And setting goals without working hard to reach them is a waste of time. Even if you know you're on the right track, the midnight express will run you over if you just sit there.

SET PRIORITIES

Know what's worth getting steamed up about and what can be ignored. Don't get frustrated about things that aren't important.

Turn to page 33 and make a list of your hopes, dreams, and aspirations. Put down the things you really want out of life. List them according to how important they are to *you*. Put the biggies at the top.

Study your list carefully and know exactly what's on it. Promise yourself that you won't get frustrated or upset over anything that isn't on the list. That means that if staying out in front of traffic isn't on the list, you're not going to lose your patience over drivers who cut in ahead of you, even if you think they're trying to run you off the road.

If short lines at the store and clean sidewalks aren't on your list, you're not going to get frustrated when someone pushes ahead of you or litters your walk.

If you can keep from losing your patience over little day-to-day nuisance kinds of things, you won't have to worry about losing it over the hopes, dreams, and aspirations that promise you a happy future.

WATCH OUT FOR OBSTACLES

Keep an eye out for obstacles that tend to make you frustrated. Avoid them whenever you can. But if you can't avoid them, at least know how to deal with them so you don't lose your patience.

If you get all riled up over heavy traffic, take the back roads home and avoid the freeway.

Go to movies when the lines are short. Schedule appointments when you know you can get right in.

Avoid obnoxious people who always get your dander up. Don't rise to their bait, and don't try to defend yourself when they attack. Just keep cool, listen when you have to, and keep your mind on something more pleasant.

Anticipate obstacles before you meet them. Picture them in your

MY HOPES, DREAMS, AND ASPIRATIONS

Make a list of things you really want out of life.

_____

_____

_____

_____

_____

_____

_____

_____

_____

_____

_____

_____

_____

mind's eye as you think they might appear. Work out ways of getting around them even if you never have to use those solutions in real life. Think about those obstacles from time to time so they stay fresh in your memory.

If you're well-armed and ready, those obstacles will melt before your eyes like summer butter.

DON'T GET FRUSTRATED

"God, grant me the serenity to accept the things I cannot change, the courage to change those that I can, and the wisdom to know the difference."

Reinhold Niebuhr's "Serenity Prayer" has helped millions of people deal with their frustrations. It can do the same for you.

If you get frustrated when you run into an obstacle, it's because you allow it to happen. If you don't let yourself get frustrated, you won't. It's that simple.

If you can't change an obstacle, work out some diversion or alternative course of action that will help you cope with it.

Take along a book or some handwork if you think you're going to get stuck in a long line.

Keep some cassette tapes of relaxing music in your car if you anticipate a traffic tie-up.

If you're caught empty-handed, strike up a conversation with a stranger or spend your time daydreaming.

If you let yourself get frustrated over day-to-day problems, you're going to get even more frustrated when you run into obstacles that block your pursuit of major goals and objectives.

Allowing yourself to get frustrated is like any bad habit. If you practice it in, you can practice it out. You can kick the habit if you work at it. And work you must if you don't want frustration and impatience to snuff out your hoped-for dreams and aspirations.

QUIT COMPETING

Nothing will take the wind out of your sails more than to find out—after you've been competing against other people and not winning—that the other people didn't even know they were in a contest.

Now's the time to turn things around and quit competing. Better yet, give the other person the advantage. They'll think they've died and gone to heaven. Try it, you'll like it. And you'll have fun doing it.

Let someone get ahead of you in traffic. Wave and flash them a smile. Give your tennis partner the net.

Wait until your spouse finishes the story, and then laugh with the others.

Applaud the moves of your fellow bridge players.

Compliment your business competitors whenever they come up with good products.

Coming in first is not the only key to success and happiness. Sometimes it's just as much fun and twice as rewarding to let someone else stand in the spotlight.

Hopes, dreams, and aspirations are a whole lot easier to come by if they don't come at the expense of other people. Pan your own gold, and let others work the same stream. Then join with them in savoring your successes.

BE HAPPY

An unexpected smile is like a flash of lightning in the middle of a storm. It breaks through the clouds of gloom and lights up the whole world. A smile might only last a moment, but its effect can last a lifetime.

You can do wonders when you substitute a smile for a frown, especially when you pass that smile along to someone who least expects it.

Try it on the driver who's holding up traffic.

Smile at the folks who keep you waiting.

And don't hesitate to laugh at yourself when you're impatient. Because if you take yourself too seriously, nobody else will.

One of the laws of nature says that emotions cannot exist independently from their respective physical expressions. That means you can't wear a sincere smile and feel sad at the same time. It works the other way too. You can't wear an angry frown when you're deliriously happy. So if you want to be happy, put on a smile and watch the world light up.

A happy heart is a healthy heart. The way you feel about what you're doing is going to affect the way you do it. If you're happy, you're going to reach your goals a lot sooner, make fewer mistakes, and have a ball doing it. On the other hand, if you choose to become frustrated and angry whenever you run into an obstacle, your dreams are going to fade quicker than a backseat romance.

LIGHTEN THE LOAD

Count to ten the next time you start getting frustrated. That little time delay will allow you to cool off enough to keep from losing your patience. It's an old remedy, but it still works.

Sometimes a little melody will keep you from tearing out your hair. Pick a familiar tune that has a strong recognizable beat and store it in your memory bank. Then, the next time you're about to blow a gasket, stop what you're doing, hum or whistle the melody, and tap out the beat. Your frustration will disappear before you know it and you'll be all charged up and raring to go.

Try word therapy as another alternative. It's free, easy to do, and you don't need a couch or a psychiatrist.

Certain words, when you say them out loud or let them float through your mind, can help create visual images that are calm, peaceful, and pleasant to think about.

Words like mist, hush, dawn, peace, melody, serenity, and tranquility have an amazing ability to quiet people down and eliminate frustration. Give each of them a try, or use favorite words of your own that have the same effect.

LOOSEN UP

If you want to strengthen your hand, take time to shuffle the cards. Take periodic breaks, even when you're working against a deadline. Think of the patience of the orchestra players who *have* to take a rest. And think how bad their music would sound if they didn't.

Break up long sessions by relaxing, stretching, or going for a walk. Talk to a friend, stare out the window, or get some exercise—anything to keep you from losing your patience. Chances are, when you get back to the task at hand, you'll be more efficient and you'll have avoided the agony that comes from flying off the handle.

Seek beauty in the things you do, even if it's driving through heavy traffic. Establish little rituals of pleasure like studying wheel cover designs or analyzing the placement of trees and shrubs along the highway. You might think these rituals sound silly. But they're worth their weight in gold if they can keep you from losing your patience.

LEARN FROM NATURE

Nature never hurries.

The tides go in and out, the sun rises and sets, and the seasons come and go. Prisoners doing time and children waiting for birthdays will try to make the days go faster, but it can't be done.

You can see the patience of nature everywhere you look — in the growing of a rose or the spinning of a spider's web.

Shakespeare spoke of the power of nature in *Othello*. "How poor are they that have not patience. What wound did ever heal but by degrees?"

With time and patience, the mulberry leaf turns into silk. Trees grow and bear fruit. Mountains erode from a thousand years of wind and rain.

One single, solitary beaver, working alone and patiently building a dam, can flood an entire city.

Be responsive to the power and patience of nature. Explore the simple things in life where patience abounds. Look for things in nature that produce a gentleness of spirit and serenity of mind.

Smell the flowers. Witness the beauty of sunrises and sunsets.

The patience of nature is not the same as idleness or indifference. It's active, concentrated strength. Use it.

LEARN FROM OTHERS

Look closely at people who always seem to be able to cope with their world and who never seem to lose their patience. Ask them how they do it, and then borrow their successful strategies.

While you're at it, pay close attention to people who are just the opposite. See what it is about their impatient behavior that turns you off, and then make sure you've flushed those traits out of your system.

Listen to the conversations of patient and impatient people. You'll soon see that a flapping tongue and an empty head go hand in hand.

Patient people talk because they have something to say. Impatient people talk because they have to say something.

Patient people never talk to pass time, they talk to save it. Patient people usually have something to say that others want to hear, and they know how to say it.

God gave everyone two eyes, two ears, and one tongue so they can see and hear twice as much as they say.

Think before you speak and compress as much thought as possible into the fewest number of words.

Dig into your history books and look for role models as sources of inspiration and encouragement. Study the lives of people who have recognized the power of patience. People like Benjamin Franklin who expressed his feelings in *Poor Richard's Almanac* when he wrote, "He that can have patience can have anything."

Pattern your life after people who have fulfilled their dreams and aspirations and who did it with patience and perseverance.

PERSEVERE

If an idea is worth having, it's worth nurturing.

If a dream promises an escape from mediocrity, allow it to bear fruit.

If success is your goal, pursue it with patience and perseverance.

There are no easy pathways to success. So you're bound to run into obstacles of one kind or another, no matter what road you take. But with ordinary talent and extraordinary perseverance, you can do almost anything. Patience is power. You just have to turn it loose and let it work its miracles.

If you took a brisk one-hour walk every day, it would only take you two years to cover the distance between New York and San Francisco. If you started walking an hour a day when you were 21, you would have circled the globe when you were 40.

Leo Hauser, author of the book, *Five Steps to Success*, is right when he says, "By the yard it's hard, by the inch it's a cinch."

VISUALIZE

Use your mental powers to bring your dreams and aspirations into focus. Create visual images of the things you have to do to reach your goals.

Change your viewpoint if you happen to lose sight of your dream for a moment. Try to see it again in a different light. Then approach it from a new perspective.

It's like looking through the trees at a sailboat on a lake. You have to keep moving and changing your viewpoint to keep the boat in sight. The boat will look different from different angles as it comes close or moves away. The same applies to your dream.

Your dream will change from day to day and so will you. Anticipate those changes and try to picture them in your mind's eye. See yourself as a patient person who can get around obstacles that used to drive you crazy. See yourself as the person you'd like to be. See yourself as a happy, prosperous, and very successful person.

KNOW YOUR SOFT SPOTS

Go back to page 5 to your list of things that tend to drive you up a wall and compare it with the list below. Combine the two lists and then pick out the demons that do the most damage to your peace of mind.

1. Other drivers. (slow, reckless)
2. Heavy traffic.
3. Competitive games where you lose.
4. Conditions that don't meet your expectations. (late trains or planes, detours, long lines)
5. People who keep you waiting.
6. Disorganization and sloppiness.
7. World events that seem out of control.

Now think back to the last time you lost your patience in each of those situations. Write down what you said, how you felt, and what you did about it.

Do this for each item on your combined list. Then look at what you've written and try to figure out what it was that made you so upset. Peg that, and you will have identified a soft spot.

The next thing you have to do is get rid of all of those soft spots. Otherwise you'll be like the person who's trying to drain the swamp while standing knee-deep in alligators. And no matter how strong you are in other areas, you'll have one helluva hard time trying to be patient.

KNOW YOUR DEADLINES

Learn to budget time as you would any other scarce and valuable resource.

Know what you have to do in the time you have to do it. Identify deadlines and do everything you can to meet them. But don't try to schedule every minute of every day. Life is not that precise. Just be sure you have a pretty good idea of how you're going to get through the next twenty-four hours. If you're too exact, you'll get frustrated by all the distractions that are bound to occur.

Whatever you do, don't waste time. Lost wealth can be restored through hard work. Lost health can be regained through good living. But lost time is gone forever. You'll never get it back and you may need it in a pinch.

Look for dead time, when you think you won't have anything to do. Fill it up with activities that will move you closer to your goal. It will be time well spent. Because as Lao Tzu, the Chinese philosopher once said, "A journey of a thousand miles begins with a single step."

If it looks like you're going to have a full day, spread things out so you'll still have time to relax.

Check your journal from time to time to see how you're spending your days. Measure your progress to make sure you're doing the things that have the highest priority.

CONQUER FEAR

Discipline yourself to do this little exercise whenever the ghosties and ghoulies are on your doorstep.

1. Ask yourself this question, "What's the worst possible thing that could happen to me if I slowed down and took my time getting through this."
2. Take a sheet of paper and write down all the things you're afraid of like getting fired, suffering penalties, not meeting deadlines, missing opportunities, or whatever. Put a star (*) by the one thing that scares you the most.
3. Gird your loins, roll up your sleeves, batten down the hatches, and get yourself ready to accept the worst if it really comes to that.

4. Take that same sheet of paper and write down all the things you can think of doing that will keep you from getting clobbered.
5. Pick the solution that you think will work the best.
6. Start working on that solution immediately while you still have the courage to do it.

Here's an example of how this exercise can work.

You're due at a very important meeting. If you slow down, you'll be late. The worst thing that could happen to you if you were late would be that you would lose your job.

If you're really in danger of losing your job, you could schedule a meeting with your boss and try to get your job back. Or you could get your resume in order, contact people who know about your experience and might be willing to hire you, or move to the Sun Belt and take an early retirement.

The best option might be to meet with your boss and try to hang on to your job. So if you're going to be late, call your boss as soon as you can get to a phone and set up a time when the two of you can get together.

Follow this exercise enough times and all your anxieties about not finishing soon enough will disappear. Before you know it, you'll be a patient, easy-going person for whom success is an everyday occurrence.

It's better to run the risk of being attacked by half the evils you anticipate than to remain in cowardly listlessness for fear of what lies beyond the door.

Even a turtle can't get ahead until it sticks its neck out.

REWARD YOURSELF

Reward yourself for being patient, and before you know it, you'll get rid of a nasty habit.

The next time you're tempted to throw in the towel, back off, take a deep breath, smile, and get rid of your frustration. Then chalk up a victory in the win column and give yourself a reward.

Your rewards can be simple and inexpensive, but they should be things that are important to you.

Paste gold stars on your refrigerator door where you can see them every day. As simple as they are, they can provide just the motivation you need to keep from losing your patience or giving up on your goals.

Try something else if you don't like gold stars. But keep looking until you can identify a system of rewards that will work for you.

Just remember to reward yourself only when you earn it. And when you earn it, be sure to take it. A reward system will only work if you strictly adhere to it.

BE HUMBLE

It's always easier to look down on others than to look down on yourself. Unless, of course, you're standing on a chair.

You would be amazed at how well other people can get along without *your* frustration and hostility.

The people who hold you up in traffic and make you stand in line are not bad people. They have families, friends, and loved ones just like you do. Beating them out of the parking lot or getting ahead of them in line is not going to make them think you're better than they are. In fact, they might just think the opposite.

It's very easy to get caught up in your own desires at the expense of others when you're impatient. But if you can slow down a little bit and start showing some humility and concern for other people, you'll soon discover that your problems aren't any bigger than anyone else's.

Turn your attention away from your own frustrations and quit worrying so much about yourself. It will make it a whole lot easier to reach your goals and objectives. And it will keep your mind off problems that you might otherwise think were unsolvable.

PRACTICE BEING PATIENT

The only way you can learn to be patient—according to old sea dogs—is by going out upon the sea of life, lying to, and riding out the gales.

Be flexible. Accept the unexpected. Don't treat unanticipated obstacles like major crises.

Learn to bear life's trials and tribulations quietly and calmly. Practice doing it until you become an expert at it.

Practice living with uncertainties and doubts. Gather and analyze unfamiliar or previously unacceptable opinions. You'll be amazed at how quickly you'll strengthen your willpower when you're able to entertain two opposing thoughts and still live at peace with yourself.

Yield to others where it won't matter; in traffic, standing in line, or in other nonessential settings where you can afford to give the advantage to someone else. Practice being tolerant. Recognize what John Caspar Lavater, the Swiss theologian pointed out when he said, "They surely are most in need of another's patience who have none of their own."

Curb your desire to go faster. Drive in the slow lane. Walk instead of run. Climb the stairs instead of using the elevator. Leave early, allow extra time, and avoid the rush.

Do your Christmas shopping in August.

WRAP-UP

By this time you should have a long list of strategies that you can use to turn your dreams and aspirations into an equally long list of accomplishments. All you need now is a plan of action to put those ideas into practice. You'll find out how to develop one when you turn to Round IV.

ROUND IV

This book has taught you how important patience is in meeting life-time goals. It has illustrated some of the reasons why people fail to achieve their hopes and aspirations. And it has provided you with a list of strategies that will not only help you become patient and easygoing, but successful as well.

Now you have to turn your attention to a comprehensive plan of action that will serve your needs, put those strategies to work, and get you moving on the pathway to success.

Here are some of the things you should include in your plan of action.

1. Develop a clear understanding of what you want out of life. Make a list of goals and objectives that you want to achieve in your life-time. Commit yourself to reaching them.
2. Learn to identify the obstacles and soft spots that get you angry, frustrated, and impatient and keep you from reaching your hoped-for level of success. Picture them in your minds eye so you can recognize them whenever they pop up in front of you.
3. Learn how to deal with those obstacles and soft spots in a calm, cool, and collected manner. Study the methods used by successful people, and incorporate their techniques into your own way of doing things.

The most important thing you can learn from this book is how to be patient over little day-to-day annoyances, and then to be able to transfer those skills over to your hopes, dreams, and aspirations for the future. Do that and you'll be halfway up the ladder of success.

All you need at this point is a happy heart and a good supply of perseverance.

You've read the book. The fat lady has sung. Now it's time to get to work.

INDEX

INDEX

THE

do it!

SUCCESS

SERIES

INTRODUCTION

What do you do with a bestseller? You turn it into a series.

That's what I've done with your old favorite, *Stop Procrastinating—DO IT!*

I've expanded the subject matter, added more topics, and come up with a gold mine of potential bestsellers. They all provide 100 percent of your minimum daily requirements for success; sound ideas, hard facts, and straight talk about key issues.

The **DO IT! Success Series** has one purpose in mind—to help you get what you want out of life and be happy doing it.

Here are the first six books in the series, including a new edition of *DO IT!*. They're all written in the same clear, concise format; they're all the same size; and they're all lively, thought-provoking, easy to understand, and refreshing in their simplicity. I hope you enjoy every one.

STOP PROCRASTINATING

JAMES R. SHERMAN, PhD

STOP PROCRASTINATING – DO IT! is the flagship of the DO IT! Success Series. It uncovers the causes of procrastination, and then it provides 22 simple, straightforward techniques for breaking this lousy habit. Over 200,000 fiirst edition copies of *DO IT!* have already been sold, making it an outstanding facilitator and an international bestseller. The expanded second edition promises to be an even better companion for busy executives, harried homemakers, active college students, and anyone else who wants to get more out of life.

THE
do it!
SUCCESS SERIES

PATIENCE
PAYS
OFF

JAMES R. SHERMAN, PhD

PATIENCE PAYS OFF is a real lifesaver for people who get frustrated and angry when unexpected obstacles keep them from reaching their goals and objectives. This enlightening book describes the causes of impatience, explores the harmful effect that restless behavior can have on health and happiness, and introduces you to the magic of staying power. Its 23 patience-building techniques are guaranteed to keep you calm, cool, and collected under any conditions.

THE

do it!

SUCCESS SERIES

NO
MORE
MISTAKES

JAMES R. SHERMAN, PhD

NO MORE MISTAKES offers an amazingly simple pathway to success: it encourages you to demand the same mistake-free behavior from yourself that you expect from other people. It explains the day-to-day blunders and major screwups that scuttle good intentions and threaten lifetime goals. It guides you through 24 state-of-the-art techniques for doing things right the first time. And it shows you how to eliminate the bad habits and dumb mistakes that keep you from being a howling success.

THE

do it!

SUCCESS SERIES

PLAN
FOR
SUCCESS

JAMES R. SHERMAN, PhD

PLAN FOR SUCCESS is an indispensable reference for people who want to climb the ladder of success but don't know where to find the ladder. The book provides a clear path to a promising future by helping you find out where you want to go and what you have to do to get there. It reveals the secrets of productive planning through clear, easy-to-understand guidelines. It's a superb planning guide and a prerequisite to success in any field.

THE
do it!
SUCCESS SERIES

FAREWELL TO FEAR

JAMES R. SHERMAN, PhD

FAREWELL TO FEAR is a long-overdue confidence builder that lowers the boom on fear and kindles the flame of courage. This easy to understand book delves into the nature and significance of fear, and shows how the shackles of hesitation can keep you from living a happy and prosperous life. Time-tested guidelines provide the antidotes to fear. And uncomplicated techniques help you build the self-confidence you need to reach your hoped-for level of success.

THE
do it!
SUCCESS SERIES

BE
A
WINNER

JAMES R. SHERMAN, PhD

BE A WINNER is a book about self-esteem; that essential quality that often spells the difference between success and failure. It explains how your self-esteem can be battered and bruised through rejection and neglect. Then it offers proven techniques for building a self-concept that can withstand assault from any quarter. Its easily-understood suggestions show you how you can gain self-respect, reach your goals and objectives, and be accepted as the confident, successful, and optimistic person you have always wanted to be.

OTHER TITLES FROM PATHWAY BOOKS

☐ **HOW TO OVERCOME A BAD BACK** $5.95

This clear, concise guide for conquering back pain, which was written from a patient's perspective, has already become a steady favorite among doctors and bad-back sufferers all over the country. It's destined to become the bible of back pain for millions.

☐ **REJECTION** $4.95

This captivating book zeroes in on the leading cause of anxiety and depression, then shows its readers how they can start being happy again. It provides a tremendous boost for lovers, jobseekers, salespeople, or anyone else who's trying to survive rejection and promote acceptance.

☐ **MIDDLE AGE IS NOT A DISEASE** $3.95

This delightful book, with its amazing facts and rib-tickling humor, is the perfect gift for anyone who has hurdled the 40's barrier and is trying to cope with the mental and physical disruption of middle age.

☐ **ESCAPE TO THE GUNFLINT** $3.95

This thrilling suspense novel takes place in the Twin Cities and north woods of Minnesota. It's an exciting page turner that can't be put down until it's finished.

HOW TO ORDER

Now you can build a library of outstanding self-help books at an unbelievably low price.

The subject matter of the first six books in the DO IT! Success Series covers six major roadblocks to success: procrastination, lack of patience, avoidable mistakes, lack of planning, fear of failure, and lack of self-confidence.

These are the same common obstacles that are faced by millions of people just like you. Each book gives you an easy-to understand explanation of why the obstacles are there. But they also give you clear, concise guidelines for breaking free of the barriers and finding your way toward a successful future.

And the books are so easy to get ahold of. Just fill out the enclosed order form and send it to Pathway Books along with your check or money order. Your books will be in the mail within 24 hours.

If you're not totally satisfied with your books, send them back, and I'll give you an immediate refund. I'll still keep your name on my mailing list so you won't miss out on any news about future books.

Be sure to check the catalog inserts for news about discounts and special orders.

Pathway Books
700 Parkview Terrace
Golden Valley, MN 55416
(612) 377-1521

ORDER FORM
(Xerox and save)

Title	$	No.	Cost
Stop Procrastinating—DO IT!....	2.95 x ___	= ___	
Patience Pays Off.............	2.95 x ___	= ___	
No More Mistakes.............	2.95 x ___	= ___	
Plan For Success.............	2.95 x ___	= ___	
Farewell to Fear.............	2.95 x ___	= ___	
Be A Winner.................	2.95 x ___	= ___	
How To Overcome a Bad Back..	OUT OF PRINT	___	
Rejection....................	4.95 x ___	= ___	
Middle Age Is Not A Disease....	3.95 x ___	= ___	
Escape To The Gunflint........	3.95 x ___	= ___	

Subtotal $ _____

6% Minn. Sales Tax   + _____

1 copy	= $1.25
2-4 copies	= $1.50
5 + copies	= $1.75

→ Shipping   + _____

Total $ _____

GUARANTEE: If you're not completely satisfied with your books, send them back. I'll refund your money immediately.

SHIP TO (Please type or print clearly)

NAME:_____

ADDRESS: _____

CITY:_____

STATE:_____ ZIP:_____

PHONE: (_____) _____ ____ DATE:_____